How to Raise a Child

The Journey from Living a Single Life, Dating, Getting Married to Starting a Family

By Lita Caine

Table of Contents

How to Raise a Child

Raising a child is not an easy job. Plain and simple!

You ask why?

It's because you are responsible for this tiny human being and making sure that they grow up into a better person. However, the journey of their growth is not as small as the length of this sentence. There are various challenges you face when you are responsible for someone's upbringing: how they talk, walk, eat and behave in social gatherings.

Feels a lot doesn't it? Yes, it may all be a bit overwhelming but that's what parenting guides are for. This one will teach you everything from how to raise a happy baby to teaching them how to deal with life as they grow.

Introduction

They say that raising a child is difficult. If you ask us, you have to be more specific. Before bringing a baby into the world, you need to ensure that you are ready for this huge responsibility.

In movies, we often see that before having a baby, couples often adopt a pet to see how they can schedule their work and personal life around a furball that's now their responsibility. When it comes to kids, they are taught the importance of responsibility by giving them a pet project that involves taking care of an egg.

So, how did you conclude that you and your spouse are ready to bring a living being into this world? If you are about to argue that you have watched videos of cute babies on YouTube and felt this maternal tug, that does not count.

We are not trying to dissuade you from having a baby. However, there are just some things that need to be put out there. When you start a family, your domestic duties double. The pressure is more on mothers as they have to take a small break to get acclimated to the baby. From feeding the baby to taking care of their basic needs, dozens of sleepless nights await you and your spouse.

You both might have different parenting styles that cancel out each other out, your sex life takes a hit, and you seldom get alone time. We aren't saying that you would face the same problems after having a baby. However, if you are counting the pros and cons, it means you are not ready. Yes, it's as simple as that!

"The way we talk to our children becomes their inner voice."

— **Peggy O'Mara, former editor and publisher of Mothering Magazine**

Raising a baby and a child are two completely different things. From the moment your baby is born to when they reach an age they can follow what you are saying, the journey is not that difficult. The road that comes after that is treacherous... filled with temper tantrums and unreasonable requests. Not to mention the imaginary friends and the blanket or stuffed toy they are not ready to let go of.

The Delicacies of Raising a Child

What brings a smile to your baby's face might surprise you. Did you know that happiness is an emotion that you teach babies rather than give them? Children who are over-indulged, protected from emotional discomfort, and showered with toys are more likely to turn out as joyless, cynical, and bored teenagers.

Babies coming out of their toddler age should experience different emotions as they help them develop their inner tools, which they can use throughout life. You don't need to be a child psychologist or an expert to raise a kid. All that's required from you and your spouse is flexibility and patience.

When a baby reaches the school-going age, most parents pay attention to their extracurricular activities and grades instead of focusing on their progress. They keep a tight schedule by making sure that the child goes to school, has lunch, and gets ready for the soccer practice or ballet lesson to get there on time.

Where did teaching them good behavior and helping them develop better habits go? Don't you think those are unnecessary for raising a child so that they turn out to be a good person?

We often forget the importance of character traits such as empathy, generosity, and kindness. The most significant character trait of all is integrity. It shows parents how their child will act when no one is looking.

There's no formula to raising a child. However, the way parents interact with their offspring is what determines how the child will grow up to be.

To help you go through the steps of raising a child, we have divided this eBook into two parts. Part 1 will focus on helping you find out whether you're ready to have a baby or not and how to raise a happy one. Part 2 will focus on how parents can teach their children good behavior.

Part 1

The Learning Curve – Are You Ready?

Are You Ready to Be a Parent?

Right after you get married, something fun happens. It feels like all your family and relatives band together to ask you one question, *"So, when are you having kids?"*

It's THE news that everyone waits for with bated breath and god forbid if you tell them that you are adopting a fur baby instead. In a way, you do have babies on your brain, just not the kind you parents and in-laws are hoping for.

Just because you are receiving a certain push doesn't mean you have to take this big step. One thing that movies have taught us is that when a child is abandoned at a young age, chances of them turning out to be a good person are low.

The point of telling you this is that when kids don't receive attention, they tend to pick up habits that distort their personalities.

If you think about it, raising a puppy is equivalent to raising a kid. You need to nurture them, keep an eye on their diet, give them a good amount of time so that they can bond with you, teach them good habits, and more.

- Should the baby be breastfed or bottle-fed?
- What kind of shampoo should I use?
- What lotion or powder won't cause rashes?
- When should I start feeding solids to my child?

If there was someone who knew how to play the parenting game right then it was Lilly and Marshal. We all could learn a thing or two from them.

So, are you ready to have a baby? Let's find out:

If you are feeling nervous about having a baby then that's completely fine. That's just the fear of the unknown and you probably have it because you grew up without any siblings. Even if you didn't, you don't need to go into panic mode.

People who grow up as the eldest sibling have first-hand knowledge about what it's like to take care of a human being. Their brotherly or sisterly responsibility is to take care of their younger siblings and protect them, and that is almost like raising a child.

Beyond this, there are plenty of good books out there, not *What to Expect When You're Expecting* because the information in there will scare you, which will answer all your questions and calm down your nerves.

Changes Are Ok

When children grow, you too grow as a person. You are almost forced because you now have someone in your life that looks up to you and your spouse for directions and decisions. This is not an easy thing to adjust to because you have to give up on a lot of things.

For example, Mike and Ella are planning to have a kid. Right now, Ella drives a Chevrolet Bolt and Mike drives a bike. While talking about the changes they will have to make after the baby arrives, the question about what they will drive comes up. Ella says that Mike will have to give up the bike because its fatality rate is 5 times more than that of a car. They both mutually decide that they will sell the bike and the small car and buy an SUV.

We are only talking about your lifestyle. When it comes to your personal life, the changes are smaller but together, they make a huge difference. These changes include giving up on alcohol, not going to the bar for a couple of years, spending less on your luxuries, saving more for the future of your kid, etc. The list is endless and things keep adding to it as time passes.

You might feel you are not doing a good job but no one has the right to judge you… not even yourself. What counts is that your heart is pure and you are doing your best.

Your Heart Feels a Bit Empty

If you were asked to name a TV show that truly explained a mother-daughter bond, what would you say?

In our mind, only one comes to mind: Gilmore Girls. The relationship between Lorelai Gilmore and Rory Gilmore was one that is still talked about today. Those two girls were thicker than thieves. They liked the same things, completed each other's sentences, were goofballs, and didn't shy away from sharing their feelings. Most importantly, they always cared for one another. We can safely say that they were the embodiment of friendship goals and mother-daughter goals.

So, it might not sound so cheesy when we say this but if you have got room in your heart, you are ready to have a baby. That's because you will be sharing your soul, body, and life with this person forever. Hence, you need to be physically and emotionally prepared for the tough road ahead. Your spouse might think that your love is being divided and that often happens because one of you will be more attached to the kid.

Right now, you are probably giving your 100% to your partner. When the baby arrives, 70% of your attention will be given to the baby, and the rest of it will be spent on yourself more or less, leaving little room for your partner. So, make sure that you both understand what you will be facing. If you find a balance, you will see that life couldn't be happier.

You Witnessed a Tantrum in the Grocery Store, and You Weren't Put Off

So, how are you with kids? Do your siblings or cousins have kids who love you a lot? Do you dote on them? Do you change their diapers or help them out with homework?

If you said "Yes" to all the above, you have passed the first test. Now, let's move on to the bad parts. How many tantrums have you seen? Like the one where your nephew wanted to hold the green spoon and not the blue one or the one where a kid lying down in the store's grocery aisle was crying and screaming at his mother.

Do you still think having kids is a good idea, congratulations! You passed the second test too. Just remember: When your angel is all grown up, they will have tantrums too.

You Are Good on the Money

Let's move on to the practical side of having a baby, and by that, we mean how much have you got in the bank? Raising a baby is expensive. According to a 2015 survey by the US Department of Agriculture, the cost of raising a child is $12,980 annually. By the time the child turns 17, a middle-income couple has spent more than $284,570. This cost is beside the cost of a college education.

Here's a little preview of a newborn checklist that includes only the necessities and no luxuries:

- Lots of bibs
- Burp cloths
- Breast pump
- Milk storage containers
- Nursing pillow
- Nursing bras
- Breast pads
- Diapers
- Baby ointments
- Baby clothes
- Changing pads
- Crib
- Blanket
- Sleep sack

This is just the beginning! You will be spending money like it's going out of fashion.

So, you have successfully reached the end of this section and you are still here. We applaud your dedication and now know that your mind's made up. Good for you! Now that you are ready, you are probably looking for advice on how to raise your child and we have plenty.

Raising a Happy Baby

When that strip showed two pink lines, you were over the moon. Are you panicking now? If yes then it's completely fine and we will tell you this every step of the way because no parent knows whether what they are doing is right or wrong. They can't seek validation because parenting is done in many ways. Your views on raising children might differ from those held by other parents, and that's alright.

When it comes to babies, their happiness hinges on you. As explained earlier, happiness is an emotion that you teach your baby through your actions. Just as you do in a complex project, you will have to keep trying no matter how many times you fail.

Read the Emotions of Your Baby

As your will mature, making their journey from a newborn to a baby that is more interactive, say... at 6 months then they will become quite good at showing you when things make them upset or content. For example, their face lighting up with a huge heart-melting smile because you entered the room or wailing their lungs out because someone took their favorite toy.

One minute, your baby might be smiling and trying to talk to you in their cute language and the next, they will be crying for your attention. This trick usually happens in a matter of seconds and at first, you will be left baffled.

So, why does this happen? Well, a baby's brain is quite wavering when it comes to emotions. In the starting years, the cerebral cortex is developing, and because of the changes this development brings, the baby's responses are automatic. Since babies experience distress more easily than happiness, they cry more and giggle less. These responses will make you want to fix whatever is wrong with your baby, which will help you develop that motherly or fatherly bond with your child.

The question is: How do you figure out your baby's mood when they are crying — are they hungry, in pain, or bored? A power most women seem to have is that they are sensitive to their baby's facial expressions and cries.

For example, a physically distressed baby will cry with his eyebrows arched, and the mouth corners turned down. In anger, the face gets flushed, and the eyebrows turn down. The cries that come out of the baby are more like roars rather than wails. Let's not forget the clenched jaw. In pain, the baby tends to pause with their breath.

We all know that an upset and fearful baby is not a happy camper! Here's something that you and most parents don't know: A loud baby is a distressed baby and not an angry one. For example, the baby does not like the sharp light in the room. As the light continues to grow brighter, the baby's stress turns to anger.

These are the little things that you should know when it comes to keeping a baby happy. The good news is that babies are not in touch with their emotions when they are born. They react to a stimulus, and there's no rhyme or reason behind it.

When a baby turns 6 months old, that is when they start to acknowledge emotions. A baby will show whether they are content or not through crying or becoming clingy. This brings us to our next point:

Let Them Figure It Out

For the first 6 months, your baby needs your full attention. You need to respond to their every need. Don't worry, you are not spoiling them.

How many times have you seen older people say that don't pick up a baby too much, or they will develop the habit of staying in your arms? Well, not to worry because babies don't learn anything in the first few months. However, when the 6 months are up, you need to set a routine and some boundaries.

If your baby is crying, your first instinct would be to run to them and pick them up. If you do this every time your baby makes a noise, you are taking away their every learning opportunity. Let your baby cry for a while, and no, this does not make you heartless. This tactic will help them build endurance. As long as you are giving your baby the right amount of affection and mommy and daddy time, you won't have to worry about anything.

You are probably wondering, "I am supposed to raise a happy baby, and letting my little one cry doesn't sit well with this."

A mistake that most parents make in the early years that sometimes even extend to teen years is that they try to solve everything for their child.

If your child can't tolerate some unhappiness and distress then they won't know what struggle is. They need to learn things on their own and develop a coping mechanism. You won't always be around (yes, it's a morbid thought, especially when your baby hasn't been born yet), which is why teaching your child the necessary coping skills is important, and that means maintaining your distance and letting them get to know and experience the world.

Let's take a look at some daily habits on how to raise a happy baby:

Take Care of Yourself Too

Just because you are a parent now doesn't mean that all your attention should go to your baby. You also need to focus on yourself, your spouse, and work. Try keeping a balance between these priorities. Motherhood and fatherhood is not an easy job. It requires a lot of energy, and a happier you means a happy baby.

Make Time for Playtime

Making small changes in your routine is the best way to accommodate the rising needs of your baby. You might be surprised at how simple it is to work your way around your baby. The most important habit that you will have to schedule in your routine is playtime. This will not only keep your baby happy but also create a cheerful environment that fosters happiness.

Babies learn a lot when they play. It allows them to explore their world, and that's how they develop motor skills. A play session can be helpful, especially when you leave them on a mat. Create a stack of blocks and knock them down. Watch as your baby will laugh at your silly antics.

Talk to Them

Do you think talking to a child is important? Many parents will say yes. But do you think talking to a baby who can't understand a word you are saying is important?

We say YES!

It's a great way to cheer your baby. Moreover, by talking to your baby, you will develop a bond with them that will bring you closer to them. Little ones are quite the listeners, and your running commentary will keep them occupied.

Did you know that your random ramblings can help develop their language? So, whether you are folding laundry or changing their diaper, talk to them about something as simple as colors or animals.

Read to Them

One of the most fun habits that will enrich your baby and boost their mental health is reading a book to them. Moreover, it also allows you to raise an emotionally stable child. So, add a bookshelf in their room and allow them to read every day.

Here are a few suggestions that we think your baby will love:

- Moo, Baa, La, La, La!
- Brown Bear, Brown Bear, What Do You See?
- Goodnight Moon
- Everywhere Babies
- Where is Baby's Belly Button?
- Peek-A Who?

Make Sleep Your Priority

Sleep plays a huge role in the development of a baby. Often, new parents complain that their baby does not allow them to sleep, and that is a good concern… not just for the mother and father but the baby too.

If you are exhausted, you won't be able to take care of your baby. The best way to encourage sleep is to create a sleep schedule. For example, you can give your baby a warm bath before bedtime or hold them in your arms while sitting in a rocking chair to lull them to sleep.

You also need to prioritize naps. According to studies, babies do most of their growing when they are sleeping. So, if your baby sleeps in the car, don't try to wake them up thinking that if they sleep now, they will trouble you at night.

Babies learn new things quickly as their minds are just developing. Anything you say and do is noticed by your baby. They absorb your actions and the tenor of your voice and mimic it as they grow up. So, for example, if you are hot-tempered, your baby might grow up with a temper of their own. Hence, you need to focus on your childrearing style and ensure your baby does not pick up your negative habits.

In a way, you can say that when you smile, so does your baby. In fact, their brain becomes "wired" to smiling. Taking care of a baby is a lot of work because you are responsible for teaching them EVERYTHING. So, feeling tired and annoyed is pretty normal. However, stressing over them and then acting out because it's all too much is not. If the latter is something you start to deal with, seek out help from a professional.

Child Rearing Styles

Psychologists have been interested in child rearing styles for a while now. Their question: How do parents affect the development of a child?

How a child is raised determines their personality. This doesn't mean that a child might not have different personalities. It's just that most of the traits children have been passed down from their parents. So, if a parent is not attentive to their child, they might grow up to be introverts. If the parent is involved in the child's life, they might grow up to be confident.

Getting to the point, there are four different child rearing styles you need to know about. First, let's look at how these styles came to be:

The 4 Parenting Styles

It was in the 1960s that a psychologist decided to work on some of the previous research that had been done on parenting. It had already been established that there were different parenting styles and practices but none of the psychologists had gone any deeper.

Psychologist Diana Baumrind decided to conduct a study on around 100 pre-school age children to see their behavior. She used parental interviews, naturalistic observation, and other research methods to identify important parenting dimensions, which included the following:

- Nurturing and warm communication style
- Disciplinary strategies

- Expectations of control and maturity

Based on these factors, Baumrind concluded that parents display 1 of the 3 parenting styles. The last was added by Martin and Maccoby.

Below are the four parenting styles explained in detail:

Authoritarian Parenting

- You should look after your kids but hearing them isn't very important
- My way or highway
- You don't consider your child's feelings as valid

Do you agree with these statements?

If yes, you are an authoritarian. You believe that children should follow the rules set by parents, and when they fail to do so, they must be punished.

An authoritarian parent does not explain why they are setting the rules. They simply believe they can do anything because they are the parent. For them, it's always, "Because I said so."

You would think with the high demands these parents have, they would constantly pay attention to their child but that's not the case. They seldom talk to their child and are not very responsive to them. They just demand that their child not make any errors and behave exceptionally. If the child makes a mistake, they are punished in a harsh manner, which often leaves the child wondering what they did wrong.

As an authoritarian parent, you would be status and obedience-oriented. Your demeanor would be dictatorial and domineering.

Authoritative Parenting

- You work hard to build a positive relationship with your child
- When you set the rules, you explain the reasons behind them
- The rules are enforced when necessary and there are consequences. However, you take the feelings of your child under consideration

Do you agree with these statements?

If yes, you are authoritative. Like an authoritarian parent, you set the rules and enforce them but the system is a bit more democratic.

They believe that children should be heard when it comes to making a decision for them. Since they consider their child's feelings, they are willing to listen to them. They do expect the child to excel in every area but they provide warmth, adequate support, and feedback every step of the way.

If the child does make a mistake, they shower them with love and forgiveness instead of punishing them.

As an authoritative parent, you will monitor your child for their well-being and impart clear conduct standards. While you will be assertive, you won't be restrictive or intrusive. Your disciplinary methods will make your child grow up into a well-mannered human being.

Permissive Parenting

- You don't give consequences
- While you do set rules, you rarely enforce them
- You have little interference in your child's life because you think they will learn best without it

Do you agree with these statements?

If yes, you are a permissive parent. Your parenting style is quite indulgent, and you don't have many demands from your children.

Permissive parents hardly discipline their children because their expectations are low regarding self-control and maturity. We wouldn't say that they leave their children willy-nilly but they aren't that much involved in their life from a disciplinary standpoint. Meaning: If a child does get into trouble, their parents will simply offer some advice on how to avoid the same mistake again but not give any punishment; this is both a good and a bad thing.

As a permissive parent, you will be more responsive than demanding. You will have a lenient and non-traditional way that will allow for self-regulation. To make sure there's peace between you and the child, you will avoid confrontation. You will be very communicative and nurturing and have a relationship with your child that will lean more towards being a friend rather than a parent.

Uninvolved Parenting

- You seldom ask your child how school went or if they need any help with homework.

- You have no idea where your child goes, where they are, and who they are with.
- You don't spend any quality time with your child.

Do you agree with these statements?

If yes, you are an uninvolved parent. People who fall in this category don't make good parents because they don't interfere in their child's life or care what's happening in it. There are few to no rules, and children don't receive any guiding, parental attention, or nurturing.

As an uninvolved parent, your thinking might be that children need to face the world and see its reality, and you're not meeting their basic needs for this reason. So, we can say that you are neglectful, but that's not your intention.

For example, if a parent has substance abuse problems and mental health issues, they might not fully take care of the child. In some cases, the parent does not know about the development of the child. Along with work, managing the household, and paying bills, they get overwhelmed, which is how the child is neglected.

The impact this has on the child is that they develop self-esteem issues. They perform badly in school and exhibit behavior problems. Lastly, their happiness is fleeting, and they don't get joy when doing anything.

The Impact on Children of Parenting Styles

Parenting styles change a child in many ways. The more involved the parents are in their children's lives, the less they grow up with behavioral or confidence issues.

Here's how the parenting styles impact children:

Authoritarian Parenting: Children grow up being proficient and obedient, but their social competence, self-esteem, and happiness rank low.

Authoritative Parenting: Children grow up happy, successful, and capable.

Permissive Parenting: Children become dependent on their parents and rank low on the happiness scale. They experience problems in the future and have a hard time accepting any authority figure, leading to poor performance at school.

Uninvolved Parenting: This parenting style is ranked the lowest on all life domains. Children who grow up with uninvolved parents lack self-control, are less competent, and have low self-esteem compared to their peers.

You might have already picked a parenting style in mind thinking that's how I will bring up my child. Is it *authoritative parenting*? If it is, you've made a good choice!

Here's why:

Maintaining the Authoritative Parenting Style

Quite a few studies on this parenting style conclude that it is indeed the best method that offers desirable outcomes. However, if the approach is not taken seriously, it slides between permissive and authoritarian parenting. It's possible that you might slide to either one of the sides, and that can destroy the relationship with your child.

A parent should continue to nurture and support their child no matter what. However, you might become extra lenient with the requirements, expectations, and rules in this parenting style. Rather than remaining consistent, you will find yourself giving in when your child throws tantrums or whines.

As a result, you might switch either one of the parenting styles mentioned above, which will impact your child. If you start being a permissive parent, it will lead to your child's poor impulse control and rebelliousness. If you start being an authoritarian parent, this move might lead to low self-esteem, poor social skills, and mental health issues. Hence, you need to walk the fine line and make sure that you don't slip.

If you want to avoid the shift, you will have to take the necessary steps as an authoritative parent. These include:

- Set boundaries, reasonable expectations, and clear limits
- Be consistent when imposing reasonable consequences
- Listen to the perspective of your child on different matters
- Encourage independence
- Explain why you set the rules and limitations so that they know that your punishment will be justified if they make a mistake.
- Be adaptable and flexible.
- Respect your child's opinion and correct them if they are wrong without breaking into an argument
- Don't be a helicopter parent but do come to their rescue when you see them failing again and again and again.

Advantages of Authoritative Parenting Style

One of the biggest benefits of the authoritative parenting style is that children develop a strong emotional bond with their parents. They tend to be happier because they know they have someone who loves them and supports them.

Let's take a look at some of the other benefits:

Secure Attachment

Since authoritative parents are listeners and nurturers, their children grow up with a calm and level-headed mind. They come up with a space where their child can feel secure and safe.

In an episode of *The Tonight Show Starring Jimmy Fallon,* Will Smith said that he has created a parenting technique, what he likes to call the "Circle of Safety." In this Circle, his children can talk about anything such as a mistake they made or something bad they did, and he won't punish them for it. This Circle allowed Will and Jada Smith to connect with their child and, at the same time, make sure that they were open and honest with each other.

According to a study published by Questia on how parenting styles impact intimate relationships and how secure attachment offers a healthier relation, authoritative parenting increases a child's self-esteem, making them friendlier and boosts their confidence.

Better Coping Skills

People deal with frustration, sadness, and anger at some point. We also learn how to control our behavior and deal with these emotions and other feelings; emotional regulation comes into play here.

The Cornell Research Program on Self-Injury and Recovery defines this term as written below:

"Emotion regulation" is generally used to describe a person's ability to effectively manage and respond to an emotional experience.

Since authorities are involved in their child's life and give them equal space to flourish, their children grow up with healthy relationships.

The most common emotional regulation strategies include:

- Exercising
- Therapy
- Talking with friends
- Keeping a journal
- Meditation
- Getting adequate sleep
- Staying physically fit
- Paying attention to any negative thoughts that might occur after or before strong emotions
- Taking a break from yourself

When parents encourage and guide their children in stressful situations and help them solve problems, they form a close and unbreakable bond. A child is more likely to remember a punishment, which they didn't think they deserved. So, you need to be careful with your punishments.

Children should be taught at an early stage how to cope with obstacles. This freedom allows them to self-regulate and cope with any problematic situation. As a result, children of authoritative parents are better problem solvers.

Higher Academic Performance

As a parent who is concerned about their child and gives them room to be true to themselves, authoritative parenting supports children's growth. These parents make sure that their child is getting good grades and doing their homework.

They attend parent-teacher meetings and encourage children to take part in extracurricular activities. Their expectations for school and home are consistent but age-appropriate and reasonable.

Good Behavior

The best thing about being an authoritative parent is that you don't have to be a disciplinarian. You do, however, have to set boundaries and provide appropriate consequences in case your child does not follow the rules.

This way, your child will be more cooperative. They will exhibit better behavior compared to children raised by authoritarian and permissive parents.

You might have noticed that we didn't mention uninvolved parenting anywhere because that's the worst method of them all and does not deserve any attention.

Open-Minded

As an authoritative parent, you will be willing to listen to your children and adapt to their perspectives. However, this doesn't mean that you do this in every situation. If a matter calls you to put your foot down, do it. Explaining will help your child understand why you are enforcing the rules.

And we finally come to the end of Part 1. You now know whether you are ready to have a baby or not, how to keep your baby happy, and what type of parenting style you need to adopt.

The next part will talk in detail about teaching your children good behavior as they grow.

Part 2

Look How Fast They Grow.

It All Begins

In an ideal world, a mother would rule over her children like a queen. She would tell her child to put away their toys, and they would do it. She would tell them to go to bed, and they would do it without arguing. She would tell them to be polite once and not snatch things from other children, and they would follow her command forever.

You are probably wondering where such children are found. Well, jokes aside — child rearing is not an easy job. We are not saying that children like the ones described above do not exist. However, raising them with good manners is the real problem. Sure, they will have their moments because *kids will be kids*. Still, disciplining them is a parent's right.

So, what does real discipline look like?

- Punishing them?
- Threatening them?
- Bribing them with cookies?
- Giving time-outs?

Wrong, wrong, wrong, and WRONG.

We have already talked about how different parenting styles shape a child's upbringing.

So, the secret to raising a child with good behavior is making clear what is expected from them and why from the start.

Remember, the "why" is important. Your children need to know why you are imposing restrictions as they grow older. It might be for their safety. Maybe, what they are asking for is not possible or wrong.

Once a child understands the limits they need to stay within, one look from a parent would be enough to let them know they need to behave properly.

This might sound easy to you, but your child begins to internalize your expectations when you lay down the ground rules. As a result, their expectations match yours. No matter how young or old your child is, they have this innate need to please their parents, which is why they will try their best to walk the path you have given them the instructions for. An 18-month-old is responsive and empathetic to the expectations of their parents.

Now that your child is growing up, teaching them self-discipline can be a little daunting. Your focus should be on the essentials first, and the discipline should start when your child is 2-year-old. Children grasp concepts and learn discipline faster, don't resist much, and behave better at this age.

Expect Respect

We say to other people that how can you expect respect when you don't treat the person in front of you with an open heart? The same fall for kids. They will be disrespectful if you will behave with them a certain way.

Children feel whining a little would get their parents' attention and get them anything they want. They believe they are untouchable and can get away scot-free.

On the other hand, children learn to respect limits and self-regulate with a set of well-defined boundaries. Below are a few tips on how to teach your kids to respect you:

Tell Them Why

Not many parents give their children explanations for why they are expected to behave a certain way. However, we urge you to do this. Why? Because the more your child will understand why you are setting such rules, the better they will understand that what you expect from them isn't arbitrary. For example, "Your child wants you to read a bedtime story. When you are done, your child requests one more. You refuse their request and tell them to go to sleep. They close their eyes for a few minutes and then pop them open to ask you a series of "Why?" questions. When you tell them to sleep again, they refuse.

Let's change your tactic. The first time your child refused to go to sleep, you should have said, "If you don't sleep now, you won't get your 8 hours of sleep, which you need to grow up to be a healthy and strong boy." You should explain instead of indulging their behavior.

Offer Praise

Whether your child gets a good grade on their test, does their homework without any mistakes, or makes the bed after getting out of it, make sure they know how proud you are of them. A child's success should be celebrated, no matter how small or big. This recognition gives the child confidence and encouragement to do more and better. For example, your son was making his bed when you came into his room early in the morning. Here's what you should say. "Look at my big boy doing his work. I am proud of you!"

Follow Your Rules Yourself

One of the biggest reasons why children rebel is when they see parents not following their own rules. Although the rules don't apply to the parents, children feel they are being treated unjustly. For example, you came home after a hectic workday and threw your jacket on the couch when you were supposed to hang it in your closet. You were doing work when your laptop crashed, causing you to scream in anger and frustration. After eating dinner, you left your dirty dishes on the table instead of placing them in the kitchen sink.

Children pick up these habits pretty fast. They will try to copy you in every way because they adore you. So, make sure to check yourself when sitting, standing, or talking in front of your children.

Cultivate a Conscience

Let's say that your child did a bad thing, but they told you about it immediately and apologized. However, you still see them feeling a little down and guilty. Instead of minimizing their discomfort, you should let them be. Keep in mind that you should apply this tip to older kids only. That guilt they are feeling will help them learn and determine what's right and wrong.

This is a great teaching opportunity. For example, you can say, "I know you understand what you did was wrong, and now you are feeling bad, but we all make mistakes. This is how you learn and grow. Next time, you will know better."

The game of discipline is all about show and tell. It would be best if you showed your children the right way of doing things. In the process, they are bound to lean towards some of the wrong ways, and that's where your parenting comes in.

Without being a strict disciplinarian, you need to show them why their way is wrong and then tell them how to do it. The rest is up to them. Keep in mind that the more loving your relationship with your children, the faster they will learn to respect your opinions.

Teach Them Problem-Solving Skills

The way you teach your children good behavior and manners changes over time. As they grow old, their problems evolve, and so does their perspective of things. So, you need to make sure that they have the right emotional, mental, and physical tools to deal with the challenges that come their way. Some they will fail, others they will pass.

And this is why it's important to teach your children problem-solving skills that will allow them to progress in the world.

Whether it's a tough math equation or a conflict caused by toys, such problems are part of a child's life. You can't always be present to solve every problem, but you sure can teach them the way. This way, they will become successful, independent, and confident individuals.

Before we begin, let's take a look at a few key points of how one can learn problem-solving skills:

Brains Can Grow

"Your brain is like a muscle. The more you learn, the more it grows."

Fixed Mindset	Growth Mindset
My Abilities, Talents, and Intelligence Are Fixed	I Can Develop My Abilities, Talents, and Intelligence
Praise Not For	**Praise For**

Born gifted, talented, being smart, not making mistakes, fixed abilities	Effort, strategies, hard work, progress, persistence, learning from a mistake and rising to a challenge

The Power of "Yet" – Say

You can't do it <u>yet</u>.

You don't know it <u>yet</u>.

If you learn and practice, you will.

Failures and Mistakes: Learning – Say

Mistakes help you improve.

You can learn from your mistakes.

Let's see what other strategies you can try.

Ask

What did you do today that made you think hard?

What new strategies did you try?

What mistakes did you make that taught you something?

What did you try that was hard today?

As a Parent – Recognize Your Own Mindset

Be mindful of your own thinking and the messages you send with your words and actions.

Problem-Solving Skills by Age Group

As mentioned earlier, a child's ability to tackle problems changes as they grow old. For example, a 2-year-old has no concept of patience. So, when they face difficulty while solving a puzzle, they keep at it until the object falls out, while an older child is more likely to give up due to frustration.

Following are different problem-solving skills that you need to teach your kid. For ease, they have been divided into age categories.

3 to 5 Years – Show Me the Hard Part

Use Emotion Coaching

- Step 1: Name and validate their emotions.
- Step 2: Let them process their emotions.
- Step 3: Give them room to solve the problem.

Say, "Show me the hard part."

- Use a dialogue-reading technique from their favorite storybooks to solve problems.
- Solve problems with creative play.

5 to 7 Years – Tell Them to Reflect On "What Worked and What Didn't."

Teach the Problem-Solving Steps

- Step 1: What am I feeling?
- Step 2: What's the problem?
- Step 3: What are the solutions?
- Step 4: What would happen if...?

- Step 5: Which one will I try?

Solve problems with craft materials.

Ask open-ended questions:

- How can we work together to solve this?
- What do you think will happen next?

7 to 9 Years – Break Problems Into Chunks

Brainstorm together

Listen

Show them the "Broken Escalator" video and have a discussion

9 to 11 Years – Use Creative Problem-Solving

Design a game and let the children figure it out. Encourage them to find any flaws in the game and put their idea on paper.

12+ Years – Use the SODAS Method

Situation

Options

Disadvantages

Advantages

Solution

- Play chess. An analysis board game such as this will spark creative thinking.
- Teach them code. It promotes logical thinking.
- Encourage them to start meaningful DIY projects.

Earlier, we talked about the "Broken Escalator" video, often shown in schools to teach perseverance and problem-solving skills.

Here's a summary of the video:

Two people are riding an escalator. Dressed in business attire, they both are talking on their phone. Suddenly, the escalator jerks to a stop. One of the riders says, "This can't be happening."

Both of them stay still on the escalator, grumbling and complaining about how late they will be. After a while, both of them shout, "Hey, we are stuck on the escalator and need help!"

If you have never seen this video and are hearing it for the first time, then your first thought was probably, "Why didn't they walk?"

Even children would understand how easy it is for them to walk. However, their state of confusion, helplessness, and despair clouded their common sense, which often happens.

If adults can behave in such a situation, how can you expect a kid to think logically? This is why teaching your children an effective way to solve problems can shape their future in a great way.

3 Strategies for Problem-Solving

1. *Model an Effective Method for Solving Problems*

Try the "think aloud" method. When solving a problem, think loud about all the solutions. This method of sorting your ideas will show your child that you too encounter problems from time to time, and this is how you solve them.

Involve them in the process, and don't be afraid to make mistakes. Tell them that some things are out of their control, which is why they shouldn't waste their energy on them. On the other hand, those things that they can control should be kept in mind.

Things That Can Be Controlled

- My behavior
- My goals
- My efforts
- Learning from my mistakes
- Taking care of myself
- Who my friends are
- Asking for help

Things That Cannot Be Controlled

- Past mistake
- Things I have to do
- What others think
- What other say

Lead with real-life examples so that your children can implement what they learned in their life.

2. *Ask for Advice*

Children are great at giving advice. You will be surprised at how logically your child thinks, and the next minute you see them running with their underpants on their head.

By asking your children for advice, you will show them that their ideas hold great value to you. This action will help you gain their confidence.

3. *Don't Provide Them With "The Answer"*

"Tell me, I forget. Teach me, and I may remember. Involve me, and I learn."

— Benjamin Franklin

This may sound a bit odd to you and go against your caring and nurturing nature, but sometimes, you need to give room for your kid to struggle. They will fail but ultimately learn something new from their experience.

No matter what your child's age, the first thing they need to master is their emotions. For example, a child will be visibly upset when they can't open the cap of a bottle they are holding. Enraged, they might throw the bottle away or look for something else to occupy their mind.

For a 3-year-old, thinking of a logical solution is hard mid-tantrum. On the other hand, a 5-year-old might ask their mother or father to open the cap.

So, how does a parent help a child navigate the emotions they are bombarded with in difficult situations? Let's take a look at the answer:

Tell your child that there's no such thing as bad emotions. This doesn't mean that all emotions are good. They just need to *accept* them, even negative ones like sadness, frustration and anger. They all teach valuable lessons, such as how to respond and to deal with a situation.

Here's a simple yet, effective way to help your child deal with emotions:

Step #1 – Name the Emotion

Let's say that you enter the room and see one of your children upset. A moment ago, you left your sons playing with toys. Now, one is clutching a toy close to their chest, and the other is bawling his eyes out. You have got a firm grasp of the situation.

What you need to do now is validate your child's emotion and name it by saying, "I know you are upset because Andre took the toy you wanted to play with."

Step #2 – Help Them Process the Emotions

Once your child has given the emotion a name, you can guide them to a calming space. In this space, they will be able to think over what happened and whether their reaction was appropriate or not.

Step #3 – Problem Solving

The last step is to listen to your child. A brainstorming session will allow them to come up with ideas, which will distract them. However, this exercise aims not to extract them but to help them deal with their emotions. So, make sure that you stay on track and let them process till the very end.

Go With Open-Ended Questions

Another great way to help your child process their emotions and improve their creative and critical thinking abilities is to ask open-ended questions.

Here are a few examples of open-ended questions:

- How can we work together and solve this problem?
- How did you solve your problem? How did you know to do it this way?
- And what do you think will happen next if…?
- What lesson did you learn from your mistake?
- Is there something you would do differently next time?

One of the best things about open-ended questions is that it shows your child that you are invested in them and would like to know what they are going through. This will help you bond with your child and improve your relationship.

The stronger the bond, the more your child will come to you to discuss their problems or brainstorm a solution.

Teach With Natural Consequences

We all face problems in our daily lives. Some are created by our actions, and others are those "oh snap" moments, which can be very irritating. For a child, all problems look alike.

You know how they say, "For every action, there's an equal and opposite reaction?"

Well, for children, this can be a great learning moment. Just make sure that they don't get hurt while facing the consequences.

For example, you give your child $20 for a day out in the amusement park. Instead of counting their money and spending it wisely, they use it all at the shooting station. You tell them that they won't be getting any more money to teach them a lesson.

This might seem a bit harsh to some parents, but it can promote problem-solving. As a result, your child will make better choices next time.

Dealing With the Changes in Children As They Grow

As much as a child needs some guidance, so do parents. We have talked at length about how to raise a good child. Now, it's time for the parents.

What's the one thing that parents dread when raising a child?

Change.

Change is inevitable. It's difficult for children, as well as adults, to manage. Many children crave stability and structure, but sadly, not many parents can provide them.

For example, a child whose parents are going through a divorce might exhibit emotions like anger and sadness. A child who is being uprooted from their home town and is forced to go to a new school might not interact with the kids. An only child spoiled by their parents might feel threatened at the arrival of a sibling.

Such changes not only impact a parent's life but a child's too. Hence, the following tips will teach parents how to deal with life changes and then help their kids cope with them:

How Change Affects Children

Most children like routine. Whether adjusting to new friends, new school, or any change in the family, the whole process can be difficult. Like adults, children too reach differently to change. One child might be upset for months about moving away from their friend while the other might bounce back to their old self in a couple of days.

You can easily know how upset your child is when you see signs of stress and anxiety. For example, your child might not do well in the subject they love, you don't see them playing video games anymore, they are not excited about the latest movies in the series they love, etc.

You will also see the following behavioral changes in them:

- Moody
- Clingy
- Irritable
- Anxious
- Sad
- Less sociable
- Afraid

If a child is old to comprehend what is happening, they take a step backward in their behavior. They might start wetting the bed again or play with toys they thought were too childish for them.

This is why it is important to always talk to your child; ALWAYS, no matter how small the change is.

6 Ways to Help Children Grow With Life Changes

Prepare Yourself and Them

Give them time to adjust to the change.

How many times have you heard the saying, "Time is of the essence?"

When it comes to children, time flies, so it does not hold much importance; rather, patience does! You can expect your child to deal with something they just got to know about. Let's say that you invested in the stock market and experienced a huge loss; this is something that will take time for you to process. You were already prepared for the loss, but it still hit you hard.

Something as simple as changing houses is a big deal for a child. They will be losing all their friends, which can be a lot to take in on short notice. For such changes, you need to prepare your child in advance.

Know Their Concerns

Most parents are concerned with fixing whatever problem their child is facing. However, this is not the right way to teach them a life lesson. For example, your child has been given a school project to build a volcano. Several videos online show step by step how to do this. Instead of telling your child to browse YouTube and watch the video, you do the project for them. Doing the assignment for your child does not teach them anything valuable. It tells them that they should always come to you with their homework.

The struggling phase is skipped altogether, and your child becomes dependent on you.

Apply the same method when it comes to helping them process their emotions. Sometimes, all children want is empathy. Acknowledge their feelings and don't let them build a shield to block their emotions.

As said above, moving to a new place can be a lot for children. Here's what you can say to validate their feelings, "I know you are scared, and that's ok. We all get scared sometimes. Let's take a deep breath, and then we will handle this together."

A great way to help your children get familiar with their emotions is to role play with them when the traditional way of explanation does not work.

Here's a scenario to help you understand this.

Your spouse works in the army, and after spending ten years in one place, you are relocating. Your kid is anxious about the move because he has made good friends here. However, this is your spouse's last tour, which will last for five years. Your 7-year-old does not want to go and insists that he can live with his aunt. So, you try explaining to him how the move can be good for him, but the onslaught of emotions is too much for him. The one thing that concerns him the most is making new friends.

So, you say to him, "I know you have an amazing circle of friends here, but there's always room for more. If you feel anxious about going to a new school, why don't we role-play meeting new friends."

Stick to the Same Old Routine

Consistency is the key to stability, and that's what your child needs as they grow. Try your best to give them the same routine day in and out unless they ask for a change.

We see in movies parents crying tears of joy and saying, "Look how fast they grow." This is completely true. Your child's growth is directly proportional to their achievements. From their first word to when they start walking, first boo-boo, going to school, participating in a competition and winning a medal for participation, all these are accomplishments that need to be celebrated. Then come the big achievements such as ranking 1st, 2nd, and 3rd in class. These are possible only when a child has a structure in life.

Apart from this, there are small things such as mealtimes and bedtimes that should always remain consistent.

Let's take a life-changing event as an example. You get divorced, and the custody of your child is divided equally. However, your child loves spending more time with you than your partner. Instead of getting angry at them, you need to understand what's causing the attachment. Since you are co-parenting, you want your partner to have a hand in your child's upbringing too.

Always listen to your children first and try to give them a familiar environment to grow into happy, healthy adults.

Provide Connection

The closer you are to your child and vice versa, the better your relationship with them. This cannot be a one-way road! If your child does not feel the same way, your involvement in their life will make them feel as if you are trying to control them or keeping tabs on them. This is especially true in the case of teens.

So, how does a parent overcome this from a young age?

What's a concern that most children have that makes them distant from their parents?

The fear of their parents leaving! So, make sure that your child knows you are not going anywhere. When a parent is coping with new changes in their life, it often happens that they become stressed and start to neglect their child.

Saying that you should not do this is easy. Every parent goes through a different set of challenges. Instead of spending time specifically to bond with your child and making it a chore, spend your free time with them. This way, your mind will be at ease, and you will be able to give your full attention to your child.

All it takes is 10 minutes to know what's happening in your child's life. Tell them to put down the phone, make eye contact and adopt an affectionate and playful attitude while chatting with them.

Give Them Choices

Life happens, and that means growing up. When it comes to a major change, children often feel out of control. This is when you need to give them choices so they can start making their own life decisions. You are probably wondering this is too much for a 5-year-old but children at this age know what they want to wear and eat, what book they like and how to make friends.

As your child grows old, allow them to make bigger life decisions such as the following:

- How to decorate their room
- Where to eat out on the weekend
- Where they would like to go for vacation

Not all change is good; that's what we think at the moment. For example, your decision to move into a new house could be based on several reasons, such as starting a family, getting divorced, or getting a new job.

Let's tackle all of these changes:

Whether you are getting married or introducing a new member into the family, you will need a bigger house. While you have too many memories attached to your old house, you will make better ones at the new house.

Divorce is a messy process. If it turns out to be amicable, couples usually split the assets equally. Let's assume that you get the house in the divorce. While it's the house where you spend all the good memories with your spouse, it's also where it all ended. Maybe you don't want to live in the past and decide to change houses.

You got a new job in another city. It pays better and offers plenty of benefits, which your old job did not. You are close to your family in the city, but the change will help you grow.

If the same changes involve children, explaining the motive behind your decision can be a bit tricky. You can give the following explanations to your child in the above situations:

You are having your second child, and your son is upset because he thinks you are changing houses just because of the baby.

"You should be excited, Adam, that you are getting a baby brother. The new house is bigger, and you will get to decorate your room and your brother's too. He will be too small to do it on his own, so it's your responsibility to take care of his things until he is old enough."

Children love responsibility when the task at hand is fun and makes them feel loved and wanted.

For divorce, the rules are slightly different because emotions are involved. Here's what you can say:

"I know you are upset that dad/mom is no longer living with us. We might be moving to a new home, but we will get to see them every day. Think of it as a vacation that you will have every month."

Lastly, explaining money problems to your children until they are of legal age isn't something you want to do. The burden can be too much and take away their youth. Here's how to explain to your child your career move:

"I know you are upset about moving to a new place but aren't you excited that daddy/mommy got a new job? You will go to a new school, which will be bigger, you can make new friends and invite them over, and we can go to Disneyland like you always wanted."

There's no knowing how a child will react to a change. Hence, as a parent, the responsibility falls on you to help them deal with their emotions, teach them how to control their feelings, and show them how to look at the positive side.

Conclusion

Children need a secure, loving, and stimulating environment to grow. You need to fulfill their emotional, physical, and developmental needs for this to happen. When a parent develops a strong bond with their child, they can raise a good person.

However, there are things that parents should be concerned about. What every person dreads is being told they are a bad parent. The truth is: No one knows how to raise a child the right way, but there's no wrong way either. A method that might suit a parent might not suit others. Moreover, the different family dynamics also play a huge role in one's upbringing.

Most parents believe that real parenting starts when a child enters their teen years because that's when they get rebellious. However, did you know that a baby starts to process emotions just after six months? They might not be able to tell you why they are upset, but they will definitely show it. This is why they say that you as a parent need to learn what your baby's different cries say.

You automatically tap into your child's behavior when you raise a happy baby. We wouldn't say that you get the key to molding them right, but you can connect with them and establish an open line of communication. That's how you can understand their emotions and talk to them about what they are feeling.

The better a child can handle their emotions, the more they can adapt to the changes life throws at them.

Disclaimer

Copyright © Year 2022 – All Rights Reserved.

No part of this ebook can be transmitted or reproduced in any form, including print, electronic, photocopying, scanning, mechanical, or recording without prior written permission from the author.

This ebook has been written for information purposes only. Every effort has been made to make this eBook as complete and accurate as possible. However, there may be mistakes in typography or content.

The purpose of this ebook is to encourage people to invest in their lives and do things during their life that they can rejoice in going back to their old age. The author and the publisher do not warrant that the information contained in this ebook is fully complete and shall not be responsible for any errors or omissions. The author and publisher shall have neither liability nor responsibility to any person or entity concerning any loss or damage caused or alleged to be caused directly or indirectly by this ebook.